THE
COAST
· OF ·
NORTHUMBERLAND

M. SCOTT WEIGHTMAN BA

Photographs by CAROLINE CLAUGHTON ARPS

To be brought up with a bucket and spade on a beach in Northumberland, as anyone who built his first sandcastle at Beadnell or Bamburgh will affirm, is to be privileged. The coast of Northumberland is not only the best introduction to the north east of England, it is among the best introductions to life. Down the full length of the coast, from the Tweed to the Tees, the sand is smooth, the dunes are seductive, the cliffs dramatic, the castles historic. This is what a coastline should be, a place of beauty at which men and women have marvelled for centuries. New every morning is the love that people have for these shores, and Cuthbert would still recognize the place.

BRIAN REDHEAD

THE ROCKS BENEATH

Northumberland's coast has a superbly varied geological history. Deserts, deltas, volcanoes, tropical swamps and frozen wastes have all played their part in the events that have led to today's magnificent coastal scenery.

At Berwick, the cliffs north and south of the Tweed are interspersed with large stretches of sand but, south of Cocklawburn, the character of the coast changes with rocky headlands giving way to dunes and beaches.

At Cocklawburn is the Eelwell anticline. In past eras, rhythmic cycles of subsidence alternating with the accumulation of silt in shallow seas left shales, sandstones, limestones and thin coals in successive horizontal layers. Mighty forces beneath the earth folded these sedimentary strata, crushing them into ridges and troughs (anticlines and synclines). The Eelwell anticline is a classic example of such a formation.

The rocky outcrop known as the Whin Sill gives a distinctive character to the north Northumberland coastline. A sill occurs where molten lava forces its way between layers of sedimentary material, cooling to form an igneous intrusion tougher than the rocks around. Differential weathering over many centuries leaves the sill, a rocky crag high above the surrounding land. Medieval castle builders found the Whin Sill ideal as a defensive site, and both Dunstanburgh and Bamburgh castles are built on it.

The castle on Holy Island is sited on a volcanic dyke (a vertical intrusion of lava) of similar age.

The rocks of the Farne Islands form the outer part of the Whin Sill. The sheets of dolerite are 30 metres (100 ft) thick in places, and were originally connected to the mainland. The reason for separation is in doubt, but is probably the work of marine erosion combined with a post-glacial rise in sea level.

Undoubtedly the section of coast with the richest variety of geological features is the shoreline between Cullernose Point and Howick Haven, just south of Craster. Cullernose Point itself is formed from the Whin Sill, yet only 100 metres (330 ft) to the south is an upstanding dolerite dyke. The coastline here is constantly fractured by folds and faults, yielding a variety of fossils. At Rumbling Kern, faulting (the cracking under pressure of rock strata along a single plane) has enabled the sea to carve a large blowhole.

The southernmost section of the Northumberland Heritage Coast lies below Craster, terminating in Druridge Bay, a stunning 6-mile (10 km) stretch of beach and dunes.

MAIN PICTURE: The Northumberland coast is rich in geological revelations. This exposure near Howick Haven shows the coarse grains of sediments, the ripple marks of ancient seas and the current bedding structures. Fossils and plant remains are common.

ABOVE: Cullernose Point is one of the most famous landscape features in northern England. There one can study the contact area between the once-molten dolerite of the Whin Sill and the sedimentary rocks into which it intruded.

LEFT: The Eelwell anticline comprises alternate beds of hard limestones and sand-stones with soft shales and coals. There are several distinc-tive exposures at Cocklawburn near Berwick-upon-Tweed.

RIGHT: Berwick-upon-Tweed and the Northumberland Heritage Coast beyond. Holy Island can be seen in the distance.

ABOVE: A poster from the Berwick Borough Museum, housed in a former barracks. A changing programme of exhibitions traces the life of the town from ancient times to the present day.

RIGHT: The Royal Border Bridge, carrying the London–Edinburgh line, is one of the world's classic railway viaducts. Designed by Robert Stephenson, it was opened by Queen Victoria in 1850.

Situated a few miles south of the Scottish border, Berwick-upon-Tweed is a town with a superb situation, famous fortifications and magnificent bridges. The place has a rugged individuality; Berwick's history alone makes it unique among British towns – between 1173 and 1482, it was captured or sacked on no less than 14 occasions as the various quarrels between England and Scotland ebbed and flowed. Edward I realized the importance of securing a firm base in the region, ordering permanent fortifications to be built around the town in 1296. Around this time Berwick was considered to be the foremost port of England and Scotland.

In the 16th century, Sir Richard Lee was ordered by Queen Mary to improve the town's defences and the walls were completed during the reign of her sister, Elizabeth I. They cost £128,648 and were the costliest undertaking of the Elizabethan period. Today they are intact and virtually unaltered since minor changes were made in 1746. One of the greatest pleasures to be enjoyed in visiting Berwick is a walk round the town along these fine walls.

Despite the many border skirmishes of medieval times, bridges between England

and Scotland have always been vital, and Berwick stands at the lowest crossing point of the Tweed. The first road bridge, known today as the 'old bridge', was built between 1611 and 1634. The dominating Royal Border Bridge higher up the river was completed in 1850. Designed by Robert Stephenson, it is one of the finest railway viaducts in the world. The concrete 'new bridge' between the two others was built in 1928 to relieve congestion on the main A1 London to Edinburgh trunk road which then ran through the town.

Berwick has many elegant and interesting buildings. Particularly worth visiting are Holy Trinity Church, a rare Puritan-inspired church built during Cromwell's Commonwealth, and the Guildhall, formerly used as a police station, court and jail, whose 46-metre (150 ft) spire dominates the town.

ABOVE INSET: Berwick's Guildhall (1754) overlooks the 16th-century town walls, built against the effects of frequent border warfare.

BELOW: Spittal beach is popular with visitors on warm summer days. Beyond is the lighthouse on Berwick Pier (1826).

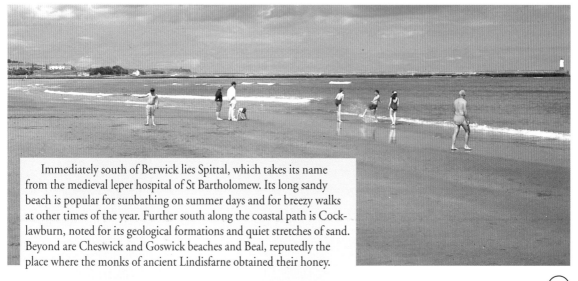

Immediately south of Berwick lies Spittal, which takes its name from the medieval leper hospital of St Bartholomew. Its long sandy beach is popular for sunbathing on summer days and for breezy walks at other times of the year. Further south along the coastal path is Cocklawburn, noted for its geological formations and quiet stretches of sand. Beyond are Cheswick and Goswick beaches and Beal, reputedly the place where the monks of ancient Lindisfarne obtained their honey.

HOLY ISLAND

Holy Island, or Lindisfarne as it was originally known, is one of the most important sites in the history of Christianity in Britain. It was here in AD635 that St Aidan founded a monastery that was to become the spiritual and educational heart of Northumbria in its 'golden age'. Here, amongst his beloved animals and birds, St Cuthbert sought respite from his missionary work. Today that same peace can still be found, for twice each day the tide sweeps across the sands, severing the link with the mainland for several hours.

The 6th and 7th centuries were a period of outstanding brilliance both for Holy Island and the whole of Northumbria. Aidan and Cuthbert travelled and preached throughout the kingdom, which became the envy of Europe. Eadfrith, Bishop-Abbot 698–721, produced with his monks the magnificent illuminated manuscripts known as the Lindisfarne Gospels. This 'golden age' was also noted for its standing stone crosses, poetry and gold metalwork – but above all for the saintliest of men.

In 793, the first Vikings came in their longboats to burn, steal and kill. Time after time they returned to ravage the holy places, and in 875 the monks were forced to flee in terror, bearing their gospels, the body of St Cuthbert and other precious relics. For 200 years the monastery remained uninhabited.

In 1082 the Benedictines revived the community, renaming Lindisfarne 'Holy Island' to commemorate the holy blood shed during the Viking invasions. The rebuilt sandstone priory remained inhabited for 450 years until Henry VIII ordered its Dissolution in 1537. The priory was once more abandoned, to become a quarry for the new castle being built on the island against possible Scots incursions.

After the union of England and Scotland in 1603 the strategic importance of the castle diminished, although it remained in use as a garrison. At the beginning of the Civil War, the castle was a Royalist stronghold but soon fell to the Parliamentarians. After a long, slow decline, the castle became a private residence in 1880, being restored by the famous architect Sir Edwin Lutyens. In 1944 the castle was given to the National Trust.

The route across the Holy Island sands used in the time of Aidan and Cuthbert remains the only access to the mainland. In 1954 the causeway was opened, forming a permanent man-made link with the mainland, and extended in 1965. Nevertheless, the tide still renders the road impassable for 2 hours before high tide and 3 hours after, and once more Lindisfarne is restored to its island status.

RIGHT: This statue of St Aidan is sited near the priory. In one hand he holds his bishop's crozier, in the other a torch symbolizing the light of the Gospel.

RIGHT: Holy Island's causeway was opened in 1954 and extended in 1965. Tide tables are provided along it to remind the unwary.

BELOW: Holy Island Castle, owned by the National Trust, stands proudly on a dolerite outcrop, Beblowe Crag.

A decorated page from St Luke's Gospel, part of the Lindisfarne Gospels, written by Eadfrith, an 8th-century Bishop of Lindisfarne, in honour of St Cuthbert. About 130 calf hides were cured to produce the vellum sheets of this famous work.

BAMBURGH

The village of Bamburgh is the ancient capital of Northumbria and the cradle of the region's history, famous for the splendid castle that dominates the coast from its crag.

Ida, the Saxon monarch and founder of the dynasty of Northumbrian kings, first built a castle here in the 6th century. In the years that followed the settlement was named 'Bebbanburgh', after Bebba, the wife of Ida's grandson. For a thousand years the castle and its people were destined to be beset by feuds and war.

King Oswald, a convert to Christianity, spent some of his early years in exile on the Scottish island of Iona. When he regained the Northumbrian throne, he sent to the monastery there for monks to spread the gospel throughout his lands. In AD635, Aidan and Oswald built the kingdom's first church in Bamburgh, probably on the site of the present church, which was built between 1170 and 1230.

Like the priory on nearby Lindisfarne, the first castle suffered from Viking raids and was rebuilt in stone in the 11th century, reaching its present magnificence in 1272. Throughout medieval times it was a focal point in the struggles between England and Scotland, and also played a part in the Wars of the Roses.

In later centuries it fell into disrepair. Lord Crewe, the last of the Prince Bishops of Durham, bought the castle in 1704, creating a charity school for girls there. But the Trustees fell into financial difficulties and it was bought as a private residence in 1894 by the inventor and industrialist William, 1st Lord Armstrong. Restored to its former proud state, the castle has remained the family's home since then. It houses the only continuous link with Bamburgh's beginnings, the old draw well, hewn through 46 metres (150 ft) of solid rock.

The village of Bamburgh is the last resting place of Northumberland's most famous heroine, Grace Darling. She was born in 1815, daughter of the keeper of the Longstone lighthouse on the Farne Islands. On the night of 7 September 1838, in a severe storm, the Forfarshire, a steamship bound for Dundee with 39 passengers, was swept onto the rocks of Big Harcar, one of the Outer Farnes. Grace and her father rowed a boat through the howling gale and lashing rain to the scene of the wreck, and succeeded in rescuing nine passengers. She was claimed by tuberculosis in 1842 and was buried in Bamburgh churchyard, opposite the museum that commemorates this young woman's bravery.

RIGHT: A window commemorating St Aidan in Bamburgh parish church. Aidan died in Bamburgh in AD651.

LEFT: Bamburgh beach with the castle beyond. King Oswald of Northumbria resided at the castle and, in AD635, sent to Iona for a missionary to convert his kingdom to Christianity.

ABOVE: The full might of Bamburgh Castle on its massive basalt outcrop is shown in this aerial view.

BACKGOUND: The striking silhouette of Bamburgh Castle at dusk.

ABOVE AND LEFT: Grace Darling became one of the first victims of the popular press in 1838, being plagued with curious visitors following her heroic deed. She died at the age of 26 in 1842. Her memorial in Bamburgh churchyard stands opposite the cottage in which she was born.

THE FARNE ISLANDS

There are 28 Farne Islands in all, situated between 5 and 8 kilometres (2–5 miles) off the Northumberland coast east of Bamburgh. They exist because the resistant volcanic rock, dolerite, of which they are made, has proved to be a match for the pounding waves of the North Sea.

The islands, which are in the care of the National Trust, are a very popular destination for lovers of wildlife, for nowhere in the British Isles can such a variety of seabirds be seen in such a small area. A trip to the islands is enjoyable at any time of year, but can be particularly rewarding in May, June and July when tens of thousands of birds are roosting. The islands are the summer home of four of the five species of British tern, as well as 12 other species of seabird, including puffins, guillemots and kittiwakes.

Another notable resident of the Farnes is the grey seal, and the colony here is one of the most important in Europe. This species of seal, the rarest in the world, is the largest surviving carnivore in the British Isles.

Historically, the Farnes are associated with St Aidan and St Cuthbert, both of whom used the islands as a place to meditate in utter solitude. Also, the Northumberland heroine, Grace Darling (see pages 8–9) spent most of her short life in lighthouses here, first on Brownsman and then on Longstone.

Because of the rocky peril that awaits unlucky or ill-prepared sailors, lighthouses have always been important to the history of the islands. Even as early as the 9th century, monks kept beacons burning here, and chronicles tell us that from 1500, a fire of coal and timber was lit each evening at the top of Prior Castell's tower.

As maritime traffic increased, a new lighthouse was constructed by Trinity House on the Inner Farne in 1776 and soon after on Brownsman. In 1809 the first round-tower lighthouse with an enclosed and revolving beam was built on the Inner Farne and on 15 February 1826, the new Longstone lighthouse functioned for the first time. Leaving the cosy security of the same circular rooms that we can visit today, Grace Darling and her father rowed out into the storm that famous night in 1838.

The Farne Islands are reached via a half-hour boat trip from Seahouses. Remember though, to go adequately waterproofed, for the sea can prove quite choppy even when it looks at its most benign!

BELOW: The approachable puffin is the most amusing bird on the island. It digs its own burrow and nests in a chamber at the end.

RIGHT: The lighthouse on Inner Farne. The Farne Islands today are uninhabited except for wildlife wardens who spend the summer season working there.

The Farne Islands are easily reached by boat from Seahouses. The National Trust, who own and manage the Farnes, charge a landing fee which is not included in the price of the boat ticket.

SEAHOUSES AND BEADNELL

Fishing has been important in Seahouses and nearby North Sunderland since the 18th century, and remains so today. In 1856, 63 fishing boats were registered there, and by 1890 it was recorded that no less than 300 keelboats (strong but clumsy vessels, often with a square sail) were using the harbour to land fish. In 1909, James Ewing's best daily herring catch was 308 crans (a cran is equivalent to 0.35 tons); the total for the village that year was 22,062 crans. In 1909, over 20,000 barrels of salted herring were exported. In Victorian times, Seahouses vessels were also involved in shipping lime for agricultural use from local quarries to other British coastal ports.

Today the lime trade is no longer carried on, and the scale of fishing activity is much reduced. However, the four trawlers and five smaller fishing boats registered at Seahouses lend much charm to the attractive harbour scene.

It is this charm that attracts many visitors to Seahouses in the summer. The first seeds of a local tourist industry were sown at the turn of the century, when fisherfolk began to supplement declining incomes by offering bed and breakfast to visitors. Today, by good fortune, the attractions of the area remain largely the same as they have always been: a magnificent yet unspoiled coastline and the fact that Seahouses harbour is the embarkation point for the equally lovely Farne Islands.

A short distance south of Seahouses is the village of Beadnell, with its small west-facing harbour and magnificent sheltered sandy beach. Near the harbour are lime kilns dating from the 18th century, now used by local fishermen as a store for lobster pots.

St Ebba's Church in the centre of the village was built in the middle of the 18th century, but there have been places of worship here almost from the dawn of Christianity in Britain. An ancient chapel, discovered in 1853, dates from the 13th century and occupies the site of a 7th-century chapel built in memory of Princess Ebba, sister of Oswald, the Saxon king of Northumbria.

BELOW AND INSET: Fishing has always been important along the Northumberland coast, but today most of the boats in Seahouses cater for visitors bound for the Farne Islands.

ABOVE: Beadnell has a sandy beach and a small harbour which provides a safe haven for yachts.

LEFT: A 'must' for any visitor to Seahouses is the Olde Ship public house, to experience the unique atmosphere of its saloon and cabin bars. The pub abounds with nautical and antique pieces, including ships' figureheads, navigating instruments and artefacts from the village's fishing fleet of old.

NEWTON AND CRASTER

Newton-by-the-Sea is just over 2 miles (3km) south of Bead-nell. Although it is thought charming today, a dismissive 19th-century writer described it as 'not pretty or pleasing, but exhibiting itself to the sea as a village of pantiled cottages and stables along three sides of a square, where only the public house has an upper storey'.

In more modern times, Newton's sheltered bay has proved ideal for water sports. Behind the dunes is Newton Pool Nature Reserve, where in specially constructed bird hides the keen onlooker can observe mallard, coot, teal and swans.

To the south of Newton, the beautiful beaches of Emble-ton Bay stretch down the coast to the romantic ruin that is Dunstanburgh Castle (see page 16) and its neighbouring village of Craster.

The commercial fortunes of Craster, as with those of many other coastal havens reliant on the white fish trade, declined with the advent of large-scale trawling. However, all was not lost, for the whinstone platform thrusting into the sea nearby provides lobsters and crabs with an ideal environment in which to thrive. Now these shellfish are harvested for most of the year.

Walking up from the harbour, one soon comes to the mainstay of Craster's economy today – the kipper factory, an enterprise started by James Robson in 1905, and now carried on by his descendants. Kippers are smoked herrings. The raw fish were formerly locally caught, but now come to Craster from the ports of north-west Scotland. To smoke kippers in the traditional manner takes between 12 and 16 hours. The Robsons have never dabbled with chemicals or artificial dyes but rely entirely on natural brine and the subtle aroma of oakwood to bring out the full flavour of their fish. The season lasts from May until September.

About a mile from the village is Craster Tower, dating from the 15th century. This is the home of the Craster family, who have been associated with the area since before the Norman Conquest.

Five kilometres (3 miles) south of Craster is Howick Hall, built in 1782 for Earl Grey. Originally it was a pele tower, that is, one built in the 16th-century as a defence against Scottish raiding parties. In 1926, after a devastating fire, the hall was rebuilt and today the grounds are open to visitors, being particularly noted for their rhododendrons.

MAIN PICTURE: The sheltered bay of Low Newton is popular with water sports enthusiasts. The village is built around a square of pantiled fishermen's cottages. Dunstanburgh Castle can be seen in the distance.

BELOW: Today, the only claim to fame of sleepy Boulmer, once notorious as a haunt of smugglers, is its daily mentions in the coastal weather forecast on national radio.

LEFT: Craster has a tiny horseshoe harbour built to commemorate a member of the Craster family killed on active service in Tibet. Shellfish are the most common catch of the village fishermen.

RIGHT: Howick Hall is situated in a wooded park at the head of a scenic dene. From spring through to autumn, the splendid gardens are open to visitors.

BELOW: Craster is renowned for the Robson family's kippers. Shellfish and salmon are also smoked there.

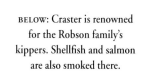

CASTLES

Northumberland has been described as the 'land of castles', and the finest of the county's fortresses grace the coast.

The castle at Holy Island stands proudly on the ancient crag 'Beblowe' and can be seen for many miles. It was built in 1539 when Henry VIII ordered that 'all havens should be fenced with bulwarkes and bloke houses aginst the Scots'. In 1639 records tell us, among other things, that there were 24 soldiers in the garrison there, and that their Captain, named Rugg, was 'known commonly by his great nose'. Between 1820 and 1880, the castle was used as a coastguard station, after which it was bought by Edward Hudson, the editor of *Country Life*, who employed Sir Edwin Lutyens to restore it. In 1944 the de Steins gave the castle to the National Trust.

From every approach Bamburgh Castle, the king of Northumbrian fortresses, stands out as the most majestic and impregnable of strongholds. The first castle there was a wooden fortress built in AD547 on the massive outcrop known as the Whin Sill. In the 11th century it was rebuilt of stone, and played a prominent part in the border wars between England and Scotland. In 1356, Edward Baliol surrendered the Scottish crown to Edward III at Bamburgh. In 1464 the castle was reputedly the first one in England to be taken by cannon fire. After lying in partial ruin for 400 years, it was bought in 1894 by William, 1st Lord Armstrong, who restored it as a family home. It is now open to the public daily between Easter and October.

Dunstanburgh Castle stands starkly on a basalt ridge overlooking Embleton Bay. It played only a peripheral part in the history of the county, being too remote from the border, and not the seat of a local lord. Built in the early 14th century by Thomas, Earl of Lancaster, it was a Lancastrian stronghold in the Wars of the Roses. The word 'stronghold' is something of a misnomer, as the castle changed hands five times during the 30 years of the wars. As artillery was used on each occasion, by 1485 Dunstanburgh lay in ruins.

Warkworth Castle, on the River Coquet, was originally a motte and bailey structure built in 1150 by Henry, son of King David I of Scotland. By the 13th century, it had grown in importance; Edward I stayed there on his way to Scotland in 1292. In 1332, Edward III granted it to Henry de Percy, who used it as a winter residence. A descendant, Henry, 1st Earl of Northumberland, built a magnificent keep and, with his son Harry Hotspur, helped to depose King Richard II in 1399. Later Earls and Dukes of Northumberland neglected Warkworth in favour of their summer home, Alnwick Castle.

LEFT: The romantic ruin of Dunstanburgh Castle. A legend relates how a young and beautiful lady was imprisoned within its walls. A knight, Sir Guy, was unable to rescue her, and his ghost is said to have spent the centuries wandering the castle in a vain search for the damsel.

ABOVE: The great hall of Bamburgh Castle, reconstructed by Lord Armstrong in the late 19th century.

LEFT: Warkworth Castle, the setting of the opening scene of Shakespeare's Henry IV, Part II.

RIGHT AND BELOW: Holy Island castle has been used as a setting for many film and television productions. It was used as Macbeth's castle in Polanski's film of Shakespeare's Scottish tragedy.

ALNMOUTH AND AMBLE

Passengers on the train racing through Northumberland towards the border may catch a glimpse of a pretty coastal village where a river winds through meadows to meet the North Sea. The river is the Aln and the village is Alnmouth, a pleasant, unspoilt seaside resort with beautiful beaches and an attractive golf course.

About 1150, William de Vesci founded Alnmouth as a seaport. In the years since then its history has been more interesting than today's sleepy appearance suggests. John Wesley visited the place in 1748, calling it 'a small seaport town famous for all kinds of wickedness'. Thirty years later it was attacked by Paul Jones, the pirate. Just to the south of the town stood the Anglo-Saxon church of St Waleric, which fell into disrepair at the beginning of the 18th century when the Aln capriciously changed its course, cutting off the church from the town.

Amble, which stands at the mouth of the River Coquet, owed its rapid development to the coal trade, but is of ancient origin as a township. There is evidence of prehistoric burial grounds on the links, and at Gloster Hill there are signs that Romans once lived there. In 1090, the priory of Tynemouth was endowed with the tithes of Amble, and a Benedictine monastery grew up there.

But that has long since disappeared and coal, not religion, came to dominate the town. The harbour was built in the mid-19th century and by 1900, the town was handling over 7,000 vessels a year. Today, Amble is Northumberland's most important fishing centre north of the Tyne, and leisure sailing has also become important. Amble Marina accommodates 200 yachts and motor cruisers. Trips around Coquet Island operate from Amble between May and June. Although landings on the island are not permitted, the trip is a must for any visitor to the town. South of Amble is Druridge Bay, the southernmost part of Northumberland's Heritage Coast.

ABOVE: Coquet Island. Its 25-metre (80 ft) lighthouse was built in 1841 on the vault of an ancient tower which guarded the island.

BELOW: Alnmouth, once the thriving outport of Alnwick, is now a peaceful seaside village.

LEFT: Amble, at the mouth of the River Coquet, was once a major coal port, but is now the biggest fishing port along Northumberland's Heritage Coast. It is also, in summer, the departure point for boats to Coquet Island. These sail around the island but do not land there.

LEFT: From this peaceful picture of boats at sunset in Amble Marina, one can easily imagine the gentle flap of rigging in the summer evening breeze. The marina was completed in 1987 to help meet the huge increase in demand for leisure sailing facilities on the north-east coast of England.

RIGHT: A crescent of sand, backed by dunes, Druridge Bay lies at the southern end of Northumberland's Heritage Coast. Plans for industrial development of this area have been thwarted.

A COASTAL HERITAGE

The rich history of Northumberland's Heritage Coast is commemorated in several museums in coastal towns and villages. The museums of Berwick tend to reflect the town's military importance during the several centuries of border warfare. The King's Own Scottish Borderers Museum relates the story of the Borderer from the Battle of Killiecrankie (1689) to the Gulf War of 1991, while the 'By Beat of Drum' museum chronicles the changing life of the British infantryman from the 16th to the 19th century. Other Berwick museums include the Borough, the Wine and Spirit and the Guildhall, which includes the old town jail.

Holy Island has two museums. The English Heritage Priory Museum covers Lindisfarne's history from the 6th century to the present day. The Museum of Island Life concentrates on the heyday of the island's fishing community.

Further south, the interesting Marine Life and Fishing Museum in Seahouses covers all aspects of life in a Northumberland coastal village while Bamburgh has the Grace Darling Museum run by the Royal National Lifeboat Institution, displaying the boat which Grace rowed on that famous stormy night.

TOP LEFT: A scene from Berwick's Borough Museum, which has items to interest all ages.

LEFT: Seahouses' Marine Life and Fishing Heritage Museum, open from Easter to October, illustrates life in a fishing village. Seven tanks display the varieties of local fish.

A dramatic picture of the famous rescue, from the Grace Darling Museum at Bamburgh.